The Science of Medicines Exploring Drug Discovery and Development

Derek Otto

Copyright © [2023]

Title: The Science of Medicines Exploring Drug Discovery and Development

Author's: Derek Otto

All rights reserved. No part of this publication may be reproduced, stored in a retrieval system, or transmitted in any form or by any means, electronic, mechanical, photocopying, recording, or otherwise, without the prior written permission of the publisher or author, except in the case of brief quotations embodied in critical reviews and certain other non-commercial uses permitted by copyright law.

This book was printed and published by [Publisher's: **Derek Otto**] in [2023]

ISBN:

TABLE OF CONTENT

Chapter 1: Introduction to Drug Discovery and Development   07

The Importance of Medicines

Historical Overview of Drug Discovery

The Drug Development Process

Chapter 2: Understanding Diseases and Therapeutic Targets   13

Disease Pathways and Mechanisms

Identifying Therapeutic Targets

Target Validation and Selection

Chapter 3: Exploring Natural Products as Medicines   19

Traditional Medicine and Ethnobotany

Isolating Bioactive Compounds

Natural Product Libraries and Screening

Chapter 4: High-Throughput Screening and Hit-to-Lead Optimization 25

Introduction to High-Throughput Screening

Assay Development and Screening Techniques

Hit-to-Lead Optimization Strategies

Chapter 5: Medicinal Chemistry and Lead Optimization 31

Structure-Activity Relationship (SAR) Studies

Medicinal Chemistry Techniques

Designing Drug-Like Compounds

Chapter 6: Preclinical Development and Safety Assessment 37

Pharmacokinetics and Pharmacodynamics Studies

Animal Models in Drug Discovery

Toxicity and Safety Assessment

Chapter 7: Clinical Trials and Regulatory Approval 43

Phases of Clinical Trials

Study Design and Patient Recruitment

Regulatory Agencies and Approval Process

Chapter 8: Post-Marketing Surveillance and Pharmacovigilance 49

Monitoring Drug Safety and Efficacy

Adverse Drug Reactions and Reporting Systems

Risk Assessment and Risk Management Plans

Chapter 9: Future Trends in Drug Discovery and Development 55

Personalized Medicine and Precision Drug Targeting

Advances in Drug Delivery Systems

Artificial Intelligence and Machine Learning in Drug Discovery

Chapter 10: Ethical Considerations in Medicinal Research 62

Informed Consent and Ethical Guidelines

Animal Testing and Alternatives

Balancing Benefits and Risks in Drug Development

Chapter 11: Conclusion: The Impact of Medicines on Society 69

Medical Breakthroughs and Improved Patient Outcomes

Challenges and Opportunities in Drug Discovery

The Role of Collaboration and Innovation in Medicinal Research

Chapter 1: Introduction to Drug Discovery and Development

The Importance of Medicines

In today's fast-paced world, medicines play a vital role in maintaining and improving our overall health. From curing life-threatening diseases to alleviating common ailments, the significance of medicines cannot be overstated. This subchapter aims to highlight the importance of medicines in our lives and shed light on their role in the field of biomedical science and biotechnology.

Medicines are a cornerstone of modern healthcare, enabling us to combat a vast array of illnesses and conditions. They are designed to target specific diseases and provide relief by either eliminating the root cause or managing symptoms. Without medicines, our ability to prevent, treat, and cure diseases would be severely limited.

One of the key aspects of medicines is their role in drug discovery and development. Biomedical science and biotechnology rely heavily on the creation and advancement of new drugs to tackle emerging health challenges. Through rigorous research and testing, scientists can develop innovative medicines that address unmet medical needs, saving countless lives in the process.

Medicines have revolutionized the treatment of chronic diseases, such as diabetes, hypertension, and asthma. They allow individuals to manage these conditions effectively, leading to improved quality of life and longevity. Additionally, medicines have played a crucial role in eradicating or controlling infectious diseases like smallpox, polio, and tuberculosis, transforming the landscape of public health.

In the field of biotechnology, medicines have opened doors to groundbreaking therapies. Biologic drugs, derived from living organisms, have revolutionized the treatment of diseases like cancer, rheumatoid arthritis, and multiple sclerosis. These innovative medicines offer targeted treatments, minimizing side effects and maximizing efficacy.

Furthermore, medicines have a significant impact on society as a whole. They not only alleviate human suffering but also contribute to economic development. By improving health outcomes, medicines enable individuals to live productive lives, contributing to the growth of communities and nations. Moreover, the pharmaceutical industry generates employment opportunities, drives research and innovation, and fosters collaborations across various scientific disciplines.

In conclusion, medicines are of paramount importance to individuals and society alike. They are instrumental in preventing, treating, and curing diseases, allowing us to lead healthier and more fulfilling lives. The field of biomedical science and biotechnology heavily relies on the development of new medicines to address health challenges and advance medical knowledge. By recognizing the significance of medicines, we can appreciate the immense impact they have on our well-being and the progress of society as a whole.

Historical Overview of Drug Discovery

Introduction:
The field of drug discovery and development has greatly advanced over the years, leading to numerous breakthroughs in medicine that have revolutionized healthcare. This subchapter provides a historical overview of drug discovery, tracing its origins to ancient times and highlighting key milestones that have shaped the field. Whether you are a student of biomedical science, a professional in biotechnology, or simply interested in the fascinating world of medicine, this chapter will give you a glimpse into the rich history of drug discovery.

Ancient Origins:
Drug discovery can be traced back to ancient civilizations, where healers and shamans relied on natural substances such as plants, herbs, and minerals to treat various ailments. These early practices laid the foundation for the use of medicinal plants and the belief in the healing properties of certain substances.

Scientific Revolution and Beyond:
The scientific revolution in the 17th century marked a turning point in drug discovery. Scientists began to explore the chemical composition of plants and minerals, leading to the isolation of active compounds. For example, the discovery of quinine from the bark of the cinchona tree revolutionized the treatment of malaria.

Industrial Revolution and Drug Development:
The industrial revolution brought about significant advancements in drug discovery and development. The synthesis of organic compounds and the development of chemical analysis techniques opened up new

possibilities for drug research. This period witnessed the discovery of several important drugs, including aspirin and morphine.

Modern Era and Targeted Therapies:
In the 20th century, drug discovery underwent a paradigm shift with the emergence of targeted therapies. Scientists began to understand the molecular basis of diseases, leading to the development of drugs that specifically target disease-causing molecules. This approach revolutionized the treatment of various diseases, including cancer, HIV/AIDS, and autoimmune disorders.

Technological Advances and Future Prospects:
Today, drug discovery is driven by cutting-edge technologies such as high-throughput screening, computer-aided drug design, and genomics. These advancements have accelerated the drug discovery process, allowing scientists to identify potential drug candidates more efficiently. Additionally, personalized medicine and gene therapies hold great promise for the future of drug discovery, offering tailored treatment options based on an individual's genetic makeup.

Conclusion:
The historical overview of drug discovery underscores the remarkable progress made in the field. From ancient remedies to modern targeted therapies, drug discovery has come a long way. This chapter provides a glimpse into the fascinating journey of drug discovery and sets the stage for exploring the intricacies of drug development in subsequent chapters. Whether you are a student or professional in the biomedical science or biotechnology field, this overview will deepen your understanding of the science behind medicines.

The Drug Development Process

In the field of biomedical science and biotechnology, the drug development process plays a crucial role in bringing new medicines to the market. It is a complex and rigorous journey that involves multiple stages, starting from the initial discovery of a potential drug molecule to its final approval by regulatory authorities. This subchapter aims to provide a comprehensive overview of the drug development process, shedding light on the various steps involved and the challenges faced along the way.

The journey begins with the identification of a potential drug target, which could be a specific protein, enzyme, or receptor involved in a disease process. Scientists then embark on a rigorous process of drug discovery, using various techniques to identify or design molecules that can interact with the target in a specific and potent manner. This stage often involves high-throughput screening, computational modeling, and medicinal chemistry to optimize the drug candidate's properties.

Once a promising drug candidate is identified, it undergoes preclinical testing, which involves extensive laboratory experiments and animal studies to assess its safety, efficacy, and pharmacokinetics. These studies help researchers understand the drug's behavior in the body, its toxicity profile, and its potential side effects. The data generated during this stage is crucial in determining whether the drug should progress to clinical trials.

Clinical trials are the next critical step in the drug development process. Divided into three phases, these trials involve testing the drug in humans to evaluate its safety, effectiveness, and optimal dosage. Phase I trials focus on determining the drug's safety profile, while Phase II trials investigate its efficacy in a larger patient population. Finally, Phase III trials involve a larger number of patients and aim to confirm the drug's benefits, monitor side effects, and compare it to existing treatment options.

Once clinical trials are successfully completed, the drug developer submits a New Drug Application (NDA) to regulatory authorities such as the Food and Drug Administration (FDA) in the United States. The regulatory agency then evaluates the data provided and decides whether to approve the drug for marketing and distribution. Post-approval, Phase IV trials may be conducted to monitor the drug's long-term safety and effectiveness in real-world settings.

The drug development process is both time-consuming and costly, often taking several years and millions of dollars to bring a new medicine to market. However, it is a necessary and essential process to ensure that new drugs are safe, effective, and beneficial to patients. By understanding the intricacies of drug development, we can appreciate the immense effort put into discovering and developing the medicines that improve and save lives.

Chapter 2: Understanding Diseases and Therapeutic Targets

Disease Pathways and Mechanisms

In the fascinating world of biomedical science and biotechnology, understanding the pathways and mechanisms of diseases is crucial for the development of effective medicines. This subchapter delves into the intricate web of disease progression, exploring the underlying mechanisms that drive illness and how researchers work to unravel these mysteries.

Diseases are complex and multifaceted, often involving a cascade of events that disrupt the normal functioning of the body. By studying disease pathways, scientists are able to identify key molecular targets and develop strategies to intervene or modulate these processes. Such knowledge forms the foundation for the discovery and development of life-saving drugs.

One of the primary focuses of disease pathway research is to identify the molecular mechanisms that initiate and perpetuate disease. For example, in cancer, scientists strive to understand the genetic mutations or alterations that drive the uncontrolled growth and spread of malignant cells. By pinpointing these molecular culprits, researchers can design drugs that specifically target and inhibit their activity, leading to more effective and personalized treatments.

Similarly, in infectious diseases, such as HIV or malaria, understanding the mechanisms by which pathogens invade and hijack host cells is critical for developing antiviral or antimicrobial drugs. By blocking these pathways, scientists can disrupt the life cycle of the pathogen and prevent its replication, ultimately halting the progression of the disease.

Furthermore, disease pathways research also involves uncovering the intricate interplay between various biological processes. For instance, in neurodegenerative diseases like Alzheimer's or Parkinson's, scientists aim to decipher the mechanisms underlying the accumulation of toxic proteins and the subsequent neuronal damage. Such knowledge allows researchers to design drugs that can either remove these toxic proteins or protect the neurons from their detrimental effects.

Advancements in technologies, such as genomics, proteomics, and imaging, have revolutionized the field of disease pathways and mechanisms. These tools enable scientists to study diseases at a molecular level, providing unprecedented insights into the intricate workings of the human body. By integrating data from these technologies, researchers can construct detailed maps of disease pathways, facilitating the identification of novel therapeutic targets.

In summary, disease pathways and mechanisms form the cornerstone of biomedical science and biotechnology. By unraveling the intricate web of disease progression, scientists can develop targeted and effective drugs to combat a wide range of diseases. Through ongoing research and technological advancements, we continue to expand our understanding of diseases, bringing us closer to innovative treatments that can improve the lives of millions worldwide.

Identifying Therapeutic Targets

In the vast field of drug discovery and development, the first crucial step is to identify potential therapeutic targets. These targets are specific molecules or pathways that play a key role in the development or progression of a disease. Identifying the right targets is essential as they serve as the foundation for designing effective drugs that can combat various diseases and improve patient outcomes.

The process of identifying therapeutic targets involves a comprehensive understanding of the underlying disease mechanisms. Scientists and researchers in the fields of biomedical science and biotechnology utilize a variety of techniques and approaches to uncover potential targets.

One common method involves studying the genetic and molecular characteristics of a disease. This can be achieved through genomic sequencing, where the entire DNA sequence of an organism or specific genes of interest are analyzed. By comparing the genetic makeup of healthy individuals with those affected by a particular disease, researchers can identify genetic variations or mutations that may contribute to the disease's development. These mutations often present themselves as potential therapeutic targets.

In addition to genomic sequencing, advanced molecular techniques such as proteomics and metabolomics are employed to identify key proteins and metabolites involved in disease pathways. By analyzing the proteins and metabolites present in diseased tissues or biofluids, researchers can pinpoint molecules that may be dysregulated or overexpressed, making them potential targets for therapeutic intervention.

Another approach to identifying therapeutic targets involves studying the cellular and molecular processes underlying a disease. This includes investigating signaling pathways, cellular receptors, and molecular interactions that contribute to disease progression. By understanding these processes, researchers can identify specific molecules that can be targeted to disrupt or modulate the disease-related pathways.

Furthermore, emerging technologies, such as high-throughput screening and computational modeling, are proving to be invaluable in the identification of therapeutic targets. High-throughput screening involves testing thousands of compounds to identify those that interact with a specific target or pathway of interest. Computational modeling, on the other hand, utilizes complex algorithms and simulations to predict the interactions between drugs and their target molecules.

In conclusion, identifying therapeutic targets is a critical step in drug discovery and development. Through a multidisciplinary approach, researchers in the fields of biomedical science and biotechnology are continuously exploring and unraveling the intricate mechanisms of diseases. By identifying and targeting these specific molecules or pathways, scientists are paving the way for the development of novel and more effective medicines to combat a wide range of diseases, ultimately improving the lives of patients worldwide.

Target Validation and Selection

In the vast landscape of drug discovery and development, one of the most critical steps is target validation and selection. A target refers to a biological molecule or pathway that plays a key role in a disease process and can be therapeutically modulated to bring about a desired effect. This subchapter aims to delve into the intricacies of target validation and selection, shedding light on its significance and the methodologies employed in this crucial stage.

Target validation is the process of verifying whether a chosen target is relevant to the disease being targeted. It involves rigorous scientific investigation to confirm the target's involvement in the disease mechanism and its potential for therapeutic intervention. This step is crucial to ensure that efforts and resources are focused on the most promising targets with the highest chances of success.

Several techniques are utilized in target validation, including genetic studies, biochemical assays, and animal models. Genetic studies involve studying the impact of genetic variations or mutations on the disease phenotype and elucidating whether they are causative factors or merely associated with the disease. Biochemical assays, on the other hand, assess the target's activity and its interaction with potential drug compounds. Animal models provide a valuable platform to investigate the effects of target manipulation on the disease phenotype, closely mimicking the human condition.

Once target validation is complete, the next step is target selection. This involves careful consideration of various parameters, such as the target's druggability, safety profile, and potential for therapeutic benefit. Druggability refers to the target's suitability for small molecule drugs or other therapeutic modalities. Safety profile evaluation involves assessing potential side effects and ensuring that the target modulation does not lead to unintended harmful consequences. The potential for therapeutic benefit is evaluated by considering the target's role in the disease mechanism, the availability of effective compounds, and the likelihood of success based on previous research.

Target validation and selection are crucial steps in drug discovery and development, as they determine the direction and success of subsequent efforts. A thorough understanding of the disease mechanism and the target's role is essential to ensure that the right target is chosen and resources are utilized effectively. By employing robust scientific methodologies and considering various parameters, researchers can maximize the chances of developing effective drugs to combat diseases.

In conclusion, target validation and selection are integral components of the drug discovery and development process. With the advent of advanced technologies and improved understanding of disease mechanisms, researchers can now make more informed decisions in identifying and prioritizing targets. This subchapter provides a comprehensive overview of target validation and selection, catering to the interests of biomedical science and biotechnology enthusiasts. Whether you are an aspiring researcher or simply curious about the science behind medicines, this subchapter will offer valuable insights into the fascinating world of drug discovery and development.

Chapter 3: Exploring Natural Products as Medicines

Traditional Medicine and Ethnobotany

Traditional medicine and ethnobotany are fields that have been deeply intertwined with human history. Before the advent of modern medicine, people relied on traditional healing practices and the knowledge of plants passed down through generations. Even today, traditional medicine continues to thrive in many cultures around the world, offering alternative approaches to health and wellness.

Ethnobotany, a branch of science that studies the relationship between people and plants, plays a crucial role in traditional medicine. It involves the exploration, documentation, and preservation of the knowledge surrounding the medicinal properties of plants. Ethnobotanists work closely with indigenous communities, learning from their traditional healing practices and gaining valuable insights into the potential therapeutic uses of plants.

Throughout history, traditional medicine has contributed significantly to the development of modern pharmaceuticals. Many widely used drugs, such as aspirin and quinine, originated from traditional remedies. By studying the medicinal plants used in traditional medicine, scientists have been able to identify and isolate active compounds that can be further developed into effective treatments.

Traditional medicine offers a holistic approach to health, focusing not only on the physical symptoms but also the emotional, spiritual, and social well-being of individuals. It often involves practices such as herbal medicine, acupuncture, massage, and meditation. These treatments aim to restore the balance within the body and promote self-healing.

While modern medicine has made tremendous advancements, traditional medicine still holds relevance in today's world. Many people continue to seek alternative therapies and herbal remedies for various health conditions. Moreover, traditional medicine can provide valuable insights into the potential mechanisms of action of natural compounds, guiding drug discovery and development.

In the field of biomedical science and biotechnology, the study of traditional medicine and ethnobotany opens up new avenues for research and innovation. Scientists can explore the vast diversity of medicinal plants and traditional remedies, identifying novel bioactive molecules that can be further developed into therapeutics. Additionally, the knowledge gained from ethnobotanical studies can inform sustainable practices for the conservation and cultivation of medicinal plants.

In conclusion, traditional medicine and ethnobotany play an important role in the field of biomedical science and biotechnology. They offer alternative approaches to health and wellness, contribute to the development of modern pharmaceuticals, and provide valuable insights for drug discovery and development. By embracing the wisdom of traditional healing practices and preserving the knowledge of ethnobotany, we can continue to explore the potential of nature's pharmacy in improving human health.

Isolating Bioactive Compounds

In the vast world of drug discovery and development, isolating bioactive compounds plays a crucial role in the search for effective medicines. These compounds are the key players responsible for the therapeutic effects of drugs and are derived from natural sources such as plants, fungi, and microorganisms. The process of isolating these compounds involves a combination of scientific techniques and rigorous experimentation.

One of the primary methods used to isolate bioactive compounds is known as bioassay-guided fractionation. This technique involves systematically separating and purifying the bioactive compounds from a natural source based on their biological activity. It begins by extracting the bioactive compounds from the source material using various solvents or extraction methods. The resulting crude extract is then subjected to a series of separation techniques, such as chromatography or crystallization, to obtain individual compounds.

Once the compounds are separated, they undergo thorough characterization using techniques like nuclear magnetic resonance (NMR) spectroscopy and mass spectrometry. These analyses help determine the chemical structure and properties of the isolated compounds, which are essential for understanding their potential therapeutic applications.

Isolating bioactive compounds is a challenging task due to the complex nature of natural sources and the presence of numerous compounds with varying levels of activity. However, advancements in technology and scientific understanding have greatly facilitated this process. Automated systems, such as high-throughput screening, allow for the rapid screening and isolation of potential bioactive compounds from large libraries of natural sources.

The isolated bioactive compounds are then further evaluated through in vitro and in vivo studies to assess their efficacy, toxicity, and mechanism of action. These studies help determine the therapeutic potential of the compounds and their suitability for drug development.

The isolation of bioactive compounds is a critical step in drug discovery, as it allows scientists to identify and study the compounds responsible for specific therapeutic effects. By isolating these compounds, researchers gain valuable insights into their structure-activity relationships and potential applications in treating various diseases.

In conclusion, isolating bioactive compounds is a complex yet essential process in the field of drug discovery and development. It involves extracting, purifying, and characterizing compounds from natural sources, followed by extensive evaluation for their therapeutic potential. This subchapter explores the techniques and challenges involved in isolating bioactive compounds and highlights the significance of this process in advancing biomedical science and biotechnology.

Natural Product Libraries and Screening

In the vast realm of drug discovery and development, scientists strive to find new and effective medicines to combat diseases and improve human health. One invaluable resource in this pursuit is the exploration of natural product libraries and screening. This subchapter delves into the significance of natural products, their libraries, and the screening process, offering insights into the world of biomedical science and biotechnology.

Natural products, derived from living organisms such as plants, animals, and microorganisms, have been used for centuries to treat various ailments. These compounds possess unique chemical structures and biological activities, making them promising candidates for drug discovery. Natural product libraries are collections of these diverse compounds, carefully curated and stored for scientific investigation.

The screening process is a crucial step in drug discovery, where scientists examine thousands of compounds from natural product libraries to identify potential drug candidates. This involves the use of high-throughput screening techniques, which enable the rapid testing of large numbers of compounds against specific disease targets. By analyzing the biological activity and therapeutic potential of these compounds, scientists can identify promising leads for further development.

The exploration of natural product libraries has yielded several notable successes in drug discovery. For instance, the discovery of the antibiotic penicillin from the fungus Penicillium notatum revolutionized the treatment of bacterial infections. Similarly, the anti-cancer drug paclitaxel, derived from the Pacific yew tree, has significantly advanced cancer therapy. These examples highlight the immense potential of natural products in the development of novel medicines.

Moreover, natural product libraries also serve as a source of inspiration for the synthesis of new compounds through medicinal chemistry. Scientists can modify and optimize the chemical structures of natural products to enhance their efficacy, reduce side effects, and improve drug-like properties. This process, known as semi-synthesis, has led to the creation of numerous life-saving drugs, including the widely used anti-malarial drug artemisinin.

In conclusion, the exploration of natural product libraries and screening is a critical aspect of drug discovery and development. This subchapter has provided a glimpse into the exciting world of biomedical science and biotechnology, showcasing the potential of natural products as sources of new medicines. As scientists continue to delve into the vast collections of natural compounds, they hold the key to unlocking future breakthroughs in healthcare and improving the lives of millions worldwide.

Chapter 4: High-Throughput Screening and Hit-to-Lead Optimization

Introduction to High-Throughput Screening

In the fast-paced world of drug discovery and development, scientists are constantly seeking innovative ways to identify potential new medicines. One such method that has revolutionized the field is high-throughput screening (HTS). This subchapter aims to introduce the concept of HTS to a diverse audience, including individuals interested in biomedical science and biotechnology.

High-throughput screening is a powerful technique that allows researchers to rapidly test thousands, or even millions, of chemical compounds for their ability to interact with target molecules. These target molecules can be proteins, enzymes, or receptors involved in disease processes. By screening large libraries of compounds, scientists can identify potential drug candidates that may have therapeutic effects.

The process begins with the creation of a compound library, which contains diverse chemical structures that have been carefully selected for their potential pharmacological activity. These compounds are then tested against a specific target in a high-throughput manner, meaning that multiple tests can be conducted simultaneously in a highly automated fashion. This allows for the screening of thousands of compounds within a short period.

The screening assays used in HTS are designed to measure the interaction between the compounds and the target molecule. These assays can be based on various principles, such as enzyme activity, receptor binding, or cell-based assays. Once the compounds have been screened, those that show promising activity are further analyzed and optimized to enhance their potency, selectivity, and pharmacokinetic properties.

High-throughput screening has revolutionized the drug discovery process by dramatically increasing the efficiency and speed of identifying potential drug candidates. It has enabled scientists to screen libraries of compounds that were previously impossible to test manually. Moreover, HTS has also facilitated the exploration of chemical space, leading to the discovery of novel drug targets and the development of innovative therapeutic approaches.

This subchapter will delve deeper into the various technologies and methodologies used in high-throughput screening. It will explore the challenges faced by scientists in implementing HTS, including compound quality, assay design, and data analysis. Additionally, it will highlight some notable success stories where HTS has played a pivotal role in the development of life-saving medicines.

Whether you are a biomedical science enthusiast or a biotechnology professional, understanding high-throughput screening is crucial in comprehending the complex process of drug discovery and development. This subchapter will serve as a comprehensive guide, equipping you with the knowledge to appreciate the impact of HTS in advancing the field of medicine and improving human health.

Assay Development and Screening Techniques

In the world of drug discovery and development, the process of identifying potential therapeutic compounds and assessing their effectiveness is a critical step. This is where assay development and screening techniques come into play. Assays are laboratory tests that enable scientists to measure the activity or performance of a compound in a controlled environment. By accurately evaluating the biological activity of potential drug candidates, researchers can make informed decisions about their potential for further development.

Assay development is the process of designing and optimizing these tests to ensure their reliability and relevance. It involves selecting appropriate biological targets, designing experimental protocols, and establishing the necessary controls to ensure accurate and reproducible results. The success of assay development lies in finding a balance between simplicity, sensitivity, and specificity. By carefully refining the assay parameters, scientists can minimize false positives and negatives, allowing for more accurate screening of compounds.

Screening techniques play a crucial role in identifying potential drug candidates from a vast library of compounds. High-throughput screening (HTS) is one such technique that allows researchers to quickly and efficiently test large numbers of compounds against a specific target. Using automation and robotics, HTS can rapidly screen thousands or even millions of compounds, significantly accelerating the drug discovery process. This technique is particularly valuable in the early stages of drug development when a broad range of compounds needs to be evaluated.

Another screening technique commonly used is virtual screening. This computational method uses computer algorithms to virtually screen large databases of compounds and predict their potential interactions with a target. By simulating the binding of compounds to the target molecule, virtual screening can quickly narrow down the list of potential candidates for further testing. Virtual screening is a valuable tool in the initial stages of drug discovery, as it saves time and resources by prioritizing the most promising compounds for experimental validation.

Assay development and screening techniques are critical components of the drug discovery and development process. They enable scientists to evaluate the potential therapeutic value of compounds efficiently and effectively. By continually refining these techniques, researchers can improve the accuracy and speed of drug discovery, ultimately leading to the development of safer and more effective medicines.

This subchapter provides a comprehensive overview of assay development and screening techniques, offering valuable insights into the world of drug discovery and development. It is a must-read for anyone interested in the field of biomedical science and biotechnology, whether they are professionals, researchers, students, or simply curious individuals.

Hit-to-Lead Optimization Strategies

In the journey of drug discovery and development, one of the critical steps is the hit-to-lead optimization process. After identifying a hit compound with promising biological activity against a particular target, the focus shifts to refining its chemical and pharmacological properties to transform it into a lead compound. This subchapter explores the various hit-to-lead optimization strategies employed in the field of biomedical science and biotechnology.

Hit-to-lead optimization is a multidisciplinary approach that encompasses medicinal chemistry, pharmacology, and computational modeling. The primary goal is to optimize the hit compound's potency, selectivity, pharmacokinetic properties, and safety profile to increase the chances of successful drug development.

One key strategy is the iterative design and synthesis of analogs, where a series of structurally related compounds are synthesized and tested to determine the structure-activity relationship (SAR). By systematically modifying different regions of the molecule, researchers can optimize its potency and selectivity against the target while minimizing off-target effects. Computational modeling techniques, such as molecular docking and quantitative structure-activity relationship (QSAR) analysis, aid in predicting the compound's binding affinity and optimizing its structure.

Another strategy involves the assessment of pharmacokinetic properties, including absorption, distribution, metabolism, and excretion (ADME). Compounds with poor ADME profiles may fail to reach the desired concentration at the target site or exhibit toxic metabolites. Therefore, structure modifications are made to improve the compound's solubility, stability, and metabolic properties, ensuring its efficacy in vivo.

Furthermore, hit-to-lead optimization strategies often involve incorporating physicochemical properties like lipophilicity, molecular weight, and hydrogen bonding capacity. These properties influence a compound's bioavailability, permeability, and interaction with biological targets. Balancing desirable properties while avoiding toxicity is essential for the successful progression of a hit compound into a lead.

Finally, safety assessment is a critical aspect of hit-to-lead optimization. Compounds must undergo rigorous testing to evaluate their potential toxic effects on various organ systems. The optimization process aims to minimize any adverse effects while maintaining therapeutic efficacy.

In conclusion, hit-to-lead optimization is a crucial stage in the drug discovery process. By employing multidisciplinary approaches, researchers can refine hit compounds into lead candidates with improved potency, selectivity, pharmacokinetic properties, and safety profiles. This subchapter provides an insight into the strategies utilized in biomedical science and biotechnology, highlighting the iterative design and synthesis of analogs, assessment of pharmacokinetic properties, optimization of physicochemical properties, and safety assessment. By understanding these strategies, readers will gain a deeper appreciation for the complex and meticulous process of transforming hit compounds into potential life-saving drugs.

Chapter 5: Medicinal Chemistry and Lead Optimization

Structure-Activity Relationship (SAR) Studies

In the world of drug discovery and development, scientists strive to understand the intricate relationship between the structure of a molecule and its biological activity. This is where Structure-Activity Relationship (SAR) studies come into play. SAR studies provide valuable insights into how the structure of a drug molecule influences its effectiveness, potency, and safety.

SAR studies involve the systematic alteration of a drug molecule's structure to evaluate its impact on various biological activities. By modifying different regions of the molecule, scientists can uncover crucial information about which structural features are necessary for the desired pharmacological effect. This information is vital for optimizing drug design and improving therapeutic outcomes.

One of the primary goals of SAR studies is to identify the key structural components responsible for a drug's activity. This knowledge allows scientists to design and synthesize more potent and selective compounds. By systematically modifying specific functional groups or substituents, researchers can determine their contribution to the overall activity. For example, by replacing a specific side chain or altering the position of a functional group, scientists can assess the resulting changes in potency or selectivity. This iterative process helps in refining drug candidates and fine-tuning their therapeutic properties.

Another important aspect of SAR studies is the identification of structural features that may lead to adverse effects or toxicity. By evaluating the relationship between the structural modifications and unwanted side effects, scientists can improve the safety profile of potential drugs. This knowledge helps in predicting and avoiding potential pitfalls during the drug development process.

SAR studies also play a crucial role in predicting the pharmacokinetic properties of a drug, such as its absorption, distribution, metabolism, and excretion (ADME). By understanding how structural modifications affect these properties, scientists can optimize a drug's bioavailability, half-life, and clearance rate. This knowledge is essential for developing drugs that can reach their target sites in sufficient concentrations and exhibit desirable pharmacokinetic profiles.

In summary, SAR studies provide valuable insights into the relationship between the structure of a drug molecule and its biological activity. By systematically modifying different regions of the molecule, scientists can uncover crucial information about the key structural components responsible for the desired pharmacological effect. Additionally, SAR studies help in predicting and avoiding adverse effects, optimizing pharmacokinetic properties, and refining drug candidates. With these insights, scientists can design and develop safer, more effective, and targeted medicines that have the potential to revolutionize the field of biomedical science and biotechnology.

Medicinal Chemistry Techniques

In the fascinating realm of drug discovery and development, medicinal chemistry techniques play a pivotal role in unraveling the mysteries of disease and finding potential cures. Harnessing the power of chemistry, these techniques provide scientists with tools to design, synthesize, and optimize compounds that could become life-saving medicines. This subchapter delves into the world of medicinal chemistry techniques, offering a glimpse into the intricate processes involved in the search for new drugs.

One of the fundamental techniques in medicinal chemistry is structure-activity relationship (SAR) analysis. This method involves investigating how changes to the chemical structure of a compound affect its biological activity. By systematically modifying the structure of a lead compound and observing its impact on efficacy and safety, scientists can optimize its therapeutic potential. SAR analysis helps guide the design of new compounds with improved properties, leading to the development of more potent and selective drugs.

Another crucial technique is high-throughput screening (HTS), which enables the rapid evaluation of thousands or even millions of compounds for their biological activity. HTS employs robotics and automation, allowing scientists to test a wide range of compounds against specific disease targets. This technique significantly accelerates the drug discovery process, increasing the chances of identifying promising hits that can be further developed into potential medicines.

The subchapter also explores the field of combinatorial chemistry, an innovative approach that involves synthesizing large libraries of diverse compounds simultaneously. By combining various building blocks and reaction strategies, combinatorial chemistry enables the creation of vast chemical libraries for screening purposes. This technique offers a vast array of potential drug candidates, allowing researchers to explore new chemical space and identify novel therapeutic options.

Furthermore, the subchapter introduces fragment-based drug design, which focuses on identifying small, low-molecular-weight compounds as starting points for drug development. By using fragments, scientists can target specific binding sites on disease-related proteins, leading to the discovery of highly potent and selective inhibitors. This approach has gained popularity in recent years due to its success in generating drug candidates with favorable drug-like properties.

Overall, the field of medicinal chemistry techniques offers an exciting glimpse into the world of drug discovery and development. By employing SAR analysis, HTS, combinatorial chemistry, and fragment-based drug design, scientists continue to push the boundaries of biomedical science and biotechnology. These techniques hold immense potential in the quest to unravel the mysteries of diseases, ultimately paving the way for the development of new and effective medicines that can improve the lives of millions worldwide.

Designing Drug-Like Compounds

In the field of drug discovery and development, the design of drug-like compounds plays a crucial role in identifying potential new medicines. This subchapter explores the fascinating world of medicinal chemistry and the key principles involved in designing compounds with the potential to become effective drugs. Whether you are a curious reader, a student of biomedical science, or someone interested in biotechnology, understanding the process of designing drug-like compounds is essential to appreciate the complexity and innovation behind the medicines we rely on.

The process of designing drug-like compounds is a multidisciplinary effort that combines knowledge from various scientific fields, including chemistry, biology, and pharmacology. The goal is to create compounds that possess specific characteristics necessary for them to interact with biological targets in the human body and elicit a therapeutic effect.

In this subchapter, we will delve into the fundamental principles that guide medicinal chemists in their quest for effective drug design. We will explore concepts such as structure-activity relationships, which involve understanding how the structure of a compound influences its biological activity. We will also discuss the importance of optimizing a compound's pharmacokinetic properties, ensuring that it can be properly absorbed, distributed, metabolized, and excreted within the body.

Furthermore, we will explore the various strategies employed in designing drug-like compounds, including the use of computational methods, high-throughput screening, and the synthesis of chemical libraries. We will discuss the benefits and challenges associated with each approach, highlighting the importance of innovation and collaboration in this field.

Throughout this subchapter, we will showcase examples of successful drug design, highlighting groundbreaking discoveries that have revolutionized the treatment of various diseases. From small molecule drugs to biologics, we will explore different types of drug-like compounds and their mechanisms of action.

By the end of this subchapter, readers from all backgrounds will gain a deeper understanding of the complexity and artistry involved in designing drug-like compounds. Whether you aspire to contribute to the field of drug discovery or simply wish to have a comprehensive understanding of the medicines that impact our lives, this subchapter will provide a valuable insight into the world of medicinal chemistry and its role in advancing biomedical science and biotechnology.

Join us on this exciting journey as we uncover the secrets behind designing drug-like compounds and learn how these innovations contribute to the development of life-saving medicines.

Chapter 6: Preclinical Development and Safety Assessment

Pharmacokinetics and Pharmacodynamics Studies

Pharmacokinetics and pharmacodynamics are two fundamental branches of study in the field of biomedical science and biotechnology that play a crucial role in drug discovery and development. Understanding how drugs interact with the body is essential for ensuring their safety and efficacy. In this subchapter, we delve into the fascinating world of pharmacokinetics and pharmacodynamics studies, shedding light on the principles and methods used to investigate the effects of drugs.

Pharmacokinetics refers to the study of how the body processes drugs. It encompasses the absorption, distribution, metabolism, and excretion (ADME) of drugs in the body. By investigating these processes, researchers can determine the optimal dosage, frequency, and route of administration for a specific drug. This knowledge is crucial for designing effective drug delivery systems and optimizing therapeutic outcomes. Pharmacokinetic studies involve measuring drug concentrations in various body compartments over time, using techniques such as blood sampling and imaging methods. These studies provide valuable insights into a drug's bioavailability, half-life, and clearance rates.

On the other hand, pharmacodynamics focuses on the study of how drugs exert their effects on the body. It explores the relationship between drug concentration and the response it produces. By investigating pharmacodynamics, researchers can determine the drug's mechanism of action, as well as its therapeutic and toxic effects. These studies often involve in vitro experiments, animal models, and clinical trials. Understanding pharmacodynamics is crucial for predicting a drug's efficacy and potential side effects, allowing for the development of safer and more targeted therapies.

Pharmacokinetics and pharmacodynamics studies are intertwined, as they contribute to a comprehensive understanding of the drug's behavior in the body. Together, they provide crucial information for drug discovery and development, helping researchers make informed decisions about dosage, formulation, and patient selection. Furthermore, these studies enable the optimization of drug therapy, ensuring maximum benefits and minimizing potential risks.

In conclusion, pharmacokinetics and pharmacodynamics studies are vital components of the drug discovery and development process. They provide essential information about how drugs interact with the body, guiding researchers in designing effective therapies. By investigating the absorption, distribution, metabolism, excretion, and effects of drugs, scientists can optimize drug therapy and improve patient outcomes. This subchapter aims to provide a comprehensive overview of pharmacokinetics and pharmacodynamics studies, offering valuable insights into the intricate world of drug development for a diverse audience interested in biomedical science and biotechnology.

Animal Models in Drug Discovery

Animal models play a crucial role in the process of drug discovery. They provide researchers with a valuable tool to understand the safety and efficacy of potential new drugs before they are tested in humans. By using animals in drug development, scientists can gather important data that helps predict how a drug may behave in the human body, allowing for safer and more effective treatments.

One of the primary reasons animal models are used in drug discovery is because of their physiological similarities to humans. Many animals, such as mice, rats, and monkeys, share genetic and biological similarities with humans, making them ideal for studying the effects of drugs on the body. By conducting experiments on animals, researchers can gain insights into how drugs are metabolized, distributed, and eliminated from the body, as well as their potential side effects.

Animal models also enable scientists to understand the mechanism of action of a drug. By observing the response of animals to a particular compound, researchers can determine how it interacts with different biological systems and identify potential therapeutic targets. This knowledge is essential in the early stages of drug development and helps guide the design of more effective drugs.

Furthermore, animal models are crucial in studying complex diseases and conditions that cannot be fully replicated in vitro. For example, diseases like cancer, Alzheimer's, and diabetes require a living system to understand their progression and response to treatment. By using animal models, scientists can mimic these diseases and test potential drug candidates in a more realistic setting, providing valuable insights into their efficacy and safety.

However, it is important to note that animal models have their limitations. No animal model can perfectly replicate the complexity of human biology, and certain differences in physiology and metabolism may affect how a drug behaves in humans. Therefore, animal models are just one part of the drug discovery process, and their findings need to be validated through clinical trials in humans.

In conclusion, animal models are indispensable tools in drug discovery and development. They provide researchers with valuable insights into the safety, efficacy, and mechanism of action of potential new drugs. Although there are limitations, animal models continue to play a vital role in advancing biomedical science and biotechnology, ultimately leading to the development of safer and more effective medicines for everyone.

Toxicity and Safety Assessment

In the world of drug discovery and development, ensuring the safety of potential medicines is of paramount importance. This subchapter delves into the crucial aspect of toxicity and safety assessment, shedding light on the rigorous processes employed to evaluate the potential harms and risks associated with new drugs.

The goal of toxicity and safety assessment is to identify any adverse effects a drug may have on the human body. This evaluation spans a range of parameters, including determining the drug's toxicity profile, its potential to cause harm in certain populations, and its long-term effects. By thoroughly understanding a drug's safety profile, researchers and regulatory authorities can make informed decisions about its potential benefits and risks.

Toxicity testing begins in the early stages of drug development, using a variety of in vitro models and animal studies. These experiments help researchers understand how a drug interacts with cells, tissues, and organs, and identify any potential toxic effects. These early studies provide valuable insights and help researchers refine the drug's formulation and dosage.

As the drug progresses through the development pipeline, further safety assessments are conducted in larger animal models, such as rats and monkeys. These studies aim to mimic the drug's effects in humans more accurately. They evaluate the drug's absorption, distribution, metabolism, and excretion, as well as its potential to interact with other drugs.

In parallel, safety assessment also examines the potential risks posed by a drug in specific populations, such as pregnant women, children, or the elderly. Factors like age, gender, and underlying health conditions can influence a drug's safety profile, and it is essential to understand these dynamics to ensure safe and effective treatment for all patients.

Toxicity and safety assessments are not limited to preclinical stages. Once a drug enters clinical trials, its safety profile is continuously monitored in human participants. Adverse events and side effects are meticulously recorded and reported, allowing researchers to refine dosage regimens and evaluate potential risks further. This ongoing assessment ensures that any safety concerns are promptly addressed and communicated to regulatory authorities.

The rigorous evaluation of a drug's toxicity and safety profile is vital to safeguarding public health. Biomedical scientists and biotechnologists play a crucial role in this process, employing cutting-edge technologies and innovative methodologies to assess the potential risks associated with new medicines. By ensuring comprehensive safety assessments, researchers, regulatory bodies, and pharmaceutical companies work collectively towards developing safe and effective treatments that can benefit everyone.

Chapter 7: Clinical Trials and Regulatory Approval

Phases of Clinical Trials

Clinical trials are a crucial part of the drug development process, designed to assess the safety and effectiveness of potential new medicines before they can be approved for use in patients. These trials are carefully conducted in multiple phases, each serving a specific purpose in the evaluation of a drug candidate. Understanding the different phases of clinical trials is essential for anyone interested in the world of biomedical science and biotechnology.

Phase 1 trials mark the initial step in testing a new drug in humans. These trials typically involve a small number of healthy volunteers and focus on assessing the drug's safety, dosage, and potential side effects. Phase 1 trials also provide valuable pharmacokinetic data, helping researchers understand how the drug is absorbed, distributed, metabolized, and excreted within the body.

Moving on to Phase 2 trials, the focus shifts to evaluating the drug's efficacy and further assessing its safety in a larger group of patients. Researchers gather data on how the drug interacts with the target disease or condition, observing its potential benefits and side effects. Phase 2 trials help determine the optimal dosage and provide information for designing more extensive studies.

Phase 3 trials are pivotal in the drug development process, involving a large number of patients across multiple sites. These trials aim to confirm the drug's effectiveness, monitor side effects, and gather additional information on its safety. Phase 3 trials often compare the new drug to standard treatments or placebos, providing robust evidence of its benefits and risks.

Once a drug successfully completes Phase 3 trials and demonstrates its safety and efficacy, the data is submitted to regulatory authorities for review. If approved, the drug can move on to Phase 4 trials, also known as post-marketing surveillance. These trials monitor the drug's long-term safety and effectiveness in a larger patient population, providing valuable real-world data.

Understanding the process and different phases of clinical trials is vital for everyone interested in the field of biomedical science and biotechnology. These trials are the backbone of drug development, ensuring that new medicines are safe and effective before they reach patients. By participating in clinical trials or staying informed about ongoing research, individuals can contribute to the advancement of medical science and the development of innovative treatments.

Study Design and Patient Recruitment

In the field of drug discovery and development, study design and patient recruitment play a crucial role in the success of clinical trials. These processes ensure that the research is conducted in a systematic and ethical manner, producing reliable results that can be used to advance medical knowledge and improve patient care. This subchapter will delve into the intricacies of study design and patient recruitment, discussing their importance and the challenges they pose.

Study design refers to the blueprint or roadmap of a clinical trial. It outlines the objectives, methods, and data collection procedures that will be employed to answer a specific research question. A well-designed study is essential as it minimizes bias, maximizes the validity of the results, and allows for meaningful interpretation. Various factors must be considered when designing a study, such as the number of participants required, the inclusion and exclusion criteria, randomization procedures, and the selection of appropriate control groups.

Patient recruitment is a critical aspect of clinical trials. The success of a study depends on the ability to recruit a sufficient number of eligible participants who are willing to participate. However, this process can be challenging due to various factors. For instance, certain medical conditions may have limited patient populations, making it difficult to find suitable candidates. In addition, social and cultural factors, fear of side effects, and logistical issues can also impact patient recruitment. It is crucial to employ effective strategies for patient recruitment, including collaborations with healthcare providers, advertising campaigns, and patient advocacy groups.

Furthermore, ethical considerations are paramount in study design and patient recruitment. Participants must provide informed consent, understanding the potential risks and benefits of participation. Additionally, the study design should prioritize patient safety and well-being, ensuring that any potential harm is minimized. Ethical guidelines, such as those provided by regulatory bodies and institutional review boards, must be followed to protect the rights of participants.

In summary, study design and patient recruitment are essential components of drug discovery and development. A well-designed study enables researchers to obtain reliable and valid results, contributing to the advancement of medical knowledge. Patient recruitment, on the other hand, ensures that studies have an adequate number of eligible participants, enabling researchers to draw meaningful conclusions. By understanding and addressing the challenges associated with study design and patient recruitment, the field of biomedical science and biotechnology can continue to make significant progress in the development of life-saving medicines.

Regulatory Agencies and Approval Process

In the world of biomedical science and biotechnology, the development and approval of medicines is a complex and highly regulated process. Regulatory agencies play a crucial role in ensuring that drugs are safe, effective, and of high quality before they are made available to the public. This subchapter will explore the various regulatory agencies involved in the approval process and shed light on the steps involved in bringing a new medicine to market.

One of the most prominent regulatory agencies is the Food and Drug Administration (FDA) in the United States. The FDA is responsible for evaluating the safety and efficacy of drugs and medical devices. They conduct rigorous reviews of preclinical and clinical data provided by pharmaceutical companies to determine whether a drug can be approved for use. Their role is to protect public health by ensuring that drugs meet the necessary standards for safety and effectiveness.

In addition to the FDA, there are regulatory agencies in other countries, such as the European Medicines Agency (EMA) in Europe and the Pharmaceuticals and Medical Devices Agency (PMDA) in Japan. These agencies have similar responsibilities and work in collaboration with the FDA to ensure that drugs meet global standards.

The approval process for a new medicine typically involves several stages. It begins with preclinical testing, where the drug is tested on animals to evaluate its safety and effectiveness. If the results are promising, the drug moves on to clinical trials, which involve testing on human volunteers. These trials are conducted in multiple phases, with each phase designed to gather specific information about the drug's safety, dosage, and efficacy.

Once the clinical trials are completed, pharmaceutical companies submit a New Drug Application (NDA) or Marketing Authorization Application (MAA) to the regulatory agency in their respective country. This application includes all the data collected during the preclinical and clinical stages, as well as information on manufacturing processes and labeling. The regulatory agency then conducts a comprehensive review of the application, considering factors such as the drug's benefits, risks, and potential side effects.

If the regulatory agency determines that the drug's benefits outweigh its risks, they will grant approval for its marketing and use. This approval comes with specific conditions and guidelines that the pharmaceutical company must follow. Post-marketing surveillance is also conducted to monitor the drug's safety and effectiveness in the general population.

Understanding the role of regulatory agencies and the approval process is crucial for anyone interested in the field of biomedical science and biotechnology. These agencies play a pivotal role in ensuring that medicines are safe and effective, providing the public with access to innovative and life-saving treatments.

Chapter 8: Post-Marketing Surveillance and Pharmacovigilance

Monitoring Drug Safety and Efficacy

In the world of medicine, ensuring the safety and efficacy of drugs is of utmost importance. The process of monitoring drug safety and efficacy involves a comprehensive and rigorous evaluation of the benefits and risks associated with pharmaceutical products. This subchapter will delve into the various aspects of monitoring drug safety and efficacy, shedding light on the essential steps taken to safeguard public health.

One of the primary goals of drug monitoring is to identify and assess the adverse effects of medications. Adverse drug reactions (ADRs) can range from mild side effects to severe allergic reactions, and monitoring them is crucial for patient safety. Regulatory bodies, such as the Food and Drug Administration (FDA) in the United States, play a significant role in monitoring ADRs by collecting data from healthcare providers, patients, and clinical trials. This data is then analyzed to determine the frequency and severity of ADRs, leading to the implementation of necessary precautions or even withdrawal of the drug from the market.

Pharmacovigilance, another critical component of drug monitoring, involves the continuous collection, analysis, and assessment of data related to the safety of medications. This process not only identifies previously unknown adverse effects but also detects patterns and trends that may emerge over time. It relies on active surveillance systems, spontaneous reporting, and electronic health records to gather relevant information. Pharmacovigilance not only protects patients from potential harm but also helps healthcare professionals make informed decisions regarding the use of specific drugs.

In addition to monitoring safety, evaluating the efficacy of drugs is equally important. Clinical trials play a vital role in determining the effectiveness of medications. These trials involve carefully designed experiments that compare the new drug against a placebo or an existing standard treatment. Researchers closely monitor various parameters, such as patient response, disease progression, and side effects, to determine if the drug achieves its intended therapeutic effect. Through these trials, scientists can ascertain the benefits of the drug and its potential limitations.

Moreover, post-marketing surveillance is crucial for monitoring the long-term safety and effectiveness of drugs once they are approved and available to the general public. This surveillance involves systematic data collection and analysis to detect any unexpected adverse reactions or changes in drug efficacy. By constantly monitoring the real-world use of medications, healthcare professionals can identify any emerging safety concerns and take appropriate actions accordingly.

In conclusion, monitoring drug safety and efficacy is a continuous and multidimensional process that ensures the well-being of patients. Through pharmacovigilance, clinical trials, and post-marketing surveillance, potential risks can be identified, and the benefits of medications can be assessed. By understanding the importance of this process, we can collectively contribute to the advancement of biomedical science and biotechnology, ultimately leading to the development of safer and more effective medicines for everyone.

Adverse Drug Reactions and Reporting Systems

In the world of medicine, the development and use of drugs play a vital role in improving human health. While drugs are designed to be safe and effective, they can sometimes have unintended effects on the human body. These unintended effects, known as adverse drug reactions (ADRs), can range from mild and tolerable to severe and life-threatening.

Understanding and managing ADRs is crucial for healthcare professionals, researchers, and patients alike. This subchapter aims to shed light on the concept of ADRs and the importance of robust reporting systems in monitoring and minimizing their occurrence.

ADRs occur when a drug, even when used correctly, causes harm to an individual. This harm can manifest as a wide range of symptoms, including allergic reactions, organ damage, or even death. It is important to note that ADRs can occur in anyone, regardless of age, gender, or medical history.

To ensure patient safety, it is imperative to have effective reporting systems in place. Reporting ADRs allows healthcare professionals and regulatory authorities to gather data and identify potential risks associated with specific drugs. This data is then used to update drug labels, provide warnings to healthcare providers, and make informed decisions regarding drug prescriptions.

One example of a reporting system is the Adverse Event Reporting System (AERS), which is used by the U.S. Food and Drug Administration (FDA). This system allows healthcare professionals, patients, and drug manufacturers to report adverse events associated with drugs. AERS plays a crucial role in detecting trends, patterns, and signals that could indicate potential safety concerns.

Another important reporting system is the Vaccine Adverse Event Reporting System (VAERS), specifically designed to monitor vaccine-related ADRs. VAERS collects and analyzes data regarding any adverse events that occur after vaccination. This system plays a vital role in ensuring the safety of vaccines and identifying any potential risks.

It is important for everyone, regardless of their background, to be aware of ADRs and reporting systems. Patients should be encouraged to report any adverse events they experience while taking medications or receiving vaccines. Healthcare professionals should be knowledgeable about ADRs, as early detection and reporting can prevent further harm. Researchers and drug developers should also actively participate in reporting systems to ensure the continuous improvement and safety of their products.

By understanding ADRs and actively participating in reporting systems, we can collectively contribute to the advancement of drug safety and patient care. It is essential to prioritize patient safety and foster a culture of open communication and reporting within the fields of biomedical science and biotechnology. Together, we can work towards a future where the benefits of medicines far outweigh their risks.

Risk Assessment and Risk Management Plans

In the field of biomedical science and biotechnology, risk assessment and risk management plans play a crucial role in ensuring the safety and efficacy of medicines. These processes are essential in every step of drug discovery and development, from the initial research phase to clinical trials and post-marketing surveillance. This subchapter aims to shed light on the importance of risk assessment and the implementation of risk management plans in the pharmaceutical industry.

Risk assessment involves the identification, evaluation, and quantification of potential risks associated with the use of a drug. It encompasses various factors such as the drug's chemical properties, mechanism of action, and potential side effects. Through extensive preclinical studies, scientists can gain insights into the drug's safety profile, its therapeutic benefits, and any risks it may pose to patients.

Once the risks are identified, risk management plans are devised to minimize or mitigate those risks. These plans outline strategies and measures to ensure that the benefits of the drug outweigh any potential harm. They include safety monitoring procedures, labeling requirements, post-marketing surveillance, and communication strategies with healthcare professionals and patients.

The implementation of risk management plans is a collaborative effort involving regulatory authorities, pharmaceutical companies, healthcare professionals, and patients. Regulatory agencies such as the Food and Drug Administration (FDA) and the European Medicines Agency (EMA) play a crucial role in evaluating the risk-benefit profile of drugs and approving their marketing authorizations. They require pharmaceutical companies to provide comprehensive risk management plans as part of the drug approval process.

Furthermore, risk management plans also involve educating healthcare professionals and patients about the potential risks associated with a drug and how to minimize them. This includes providing clear instructions on dosage, contraindications, and potential drug interactions. Patient support programs and adverse event reporting systems are also implemented to ensure that any potential risks are promptly identified and addressed.

In conclusion, risk assessment and risk management plans are vital components of drug discovery and development in the fields of biomedical science and biotechnology. They help to ensure that medicines are safe and effective for patients. By identifying and mitigating potential risks, these processes contribute to the overall improvement of public health and the advancement of medical science.

Chapter 9: Future Trends in Drug Discovery and Development

Personalized Medicine and Precision Drug Targeting

In recent years, the field of medicine has been revolutionized by the advent of personalized medicine and precision drug targeting. These groundbreaking approaches have the potential to transform the way we diagnose and treat diseases, offering tailored therapies that are highly effective and minimize adverse side effects. This chapter explores the fundamental concepts and cutting-edge technologies that underpin this exciting new era in healthcare.

Personalized medicine is a paradigm shift from the traditional one-size-fits-all approach to treatment. It recognizes that every individual is unique, with their own genetic makeup, lifestyle, and environmental factors influencing their health. By harnessing the power of genomic and molecular data, healthcare professionals can now identify specific genetic variations or biomarkers that drive diseases. This enables them to develop personalized treatment plans that target the root cause of the condition, rather than merely alleviating symptoms.

Precision drug targeting is a key pillar of personalized medicine. By understanding the molecular mechanisms underlying diseases, scientists can develop drugs that specifically target the molecules or pathways responsible for the disease. This approach offers several advantages over conventional therapies. Firstly, precision drugs are more effective as they selectively act on disease-causing targets, leaving healthy cells unharmed. This not only increases the therapeutic efficacy but also reduces the risk of adverse side effects.

Furthermore, precision drug targeting allows for the development of companion diagnostics. These tests can identify patients who are most likely to benefit from a specific therapy, enabling healthcare professionals to make informed treatment decisions. This not only improves patient outcomes but also reduces healthcare costs by avoiding unnecessary treatments.

In the field of biomedical science and biotechnology, personalized medicine and precision drug targeting present exciting opportunities for researchers and healthcare professionals. By unraveling the complex interplay between genes, proteins, and diseases, scientists can identify novel drug targets and develop innovative therapies. This requires interdisciplinary collaboration, with experts from various fields like genomics, pharmacology, and bioinformatics working together to decode the intricacies of personalized medicine.

Moreover, the implementation of personalized medicine has far-reaching implications for healthcare systems. It necessitates the integration of advanced technologies, such as high-throughput sequencing, bioinformatics, and artificial intelligence, to analyze vast amounts of genomic and clinical data. This data-driven approach enables clinicians to make evidence-based treatment decisions, leading to improved patient outcomes and a more efficient healthcare system.

In conclusion, personalized medicine and precision drug targeting are revolutionizing the field of medicine, offering tailored therapies that are highly effective and minimize adverse side effects. By harnessing the power of genomics and molecular data, healthcare professionals can develop targeted treatments that address the root cause of diseases. The field of biomedical science and biotechnology plays a crucial role in driving this transformative shift, through research, innovation, and interdisciplinary collaboration. As personalized medicine continues to evolve, it holds the promise of a future where healthcare is truly tailored to each individual, leading to improved patient outcomes and a healthier society.

Advances in Drug Delivery Systems

In recent years, there have been remarkable advances in the development of drug delivery systems, revolutionizing the way medicines are administered and improving their efficacy. These breakthroughs have paved the way for more targeted and efficient treatment options, benefiting patients across various medical fields. This subchapter explores some of the most significant advancements in drug delivery systems and their impact on biomedical science and biotechnology.

One of the most notable advancements is the development of nanotechnology-based drug delivery systems. Nanoparticles, with sizes ranging from 1 to 100 nanometers, have unique properties that make them ideal carriers for drugs. They can be engineered to encapsulate therapeutic agents and deliver them directly to specific cells or tissues, improving drug stability and reducing side effects. These nanocarriers can also be modified to release drugs in a controlled manner, ensuring a sustained and optimal therapeutic effect.

Another area of significant progress is the use of biomaterials in drug delivery systems. Biocompatible materials, such as polymers, lipids, and hydrogels, have been extensively studied and utilized to encapsulate drugs and deliver them to target sites. These biomaterial-based systems can protect drugs from degradation, enhance their solubility, and provide sustained release profiles. Moreover, these materials can be tailored to respond to specific biological cues, enabling triggered drug release at the desired location.

Advancements in drug delivery systems have also led to the development of innovative routes of administration. Traditional routes, such as oral or intravenous, often have limitations in terms of drug absorption, distribution, and targeting. However, with the advent of transdermal patches, inhalation devices, and implantable devices, drugs can now be delivered through alternative routes, enhancing patient compliance and improving therapeutic outcomes.

In addition to these technological advancements, researchers have also explored the potential of targeted drug delivery systems. By conjugating drugs with ligands or antibodies specific to disease markers, drugs can be directly delivered to diseased cells or tissues, minimizing systemic exposure and reducing off-target effects. This targeted approach holds great promise for the treatment of various diseases, including cancer, where precision and specificity are crucial.

In conclusion, the field of drug delivery systems has witnessed remarkable advancements in recent years. These breakthroughs have transformed the way medicines are delivered, improving their efficacy, safety, and patient compliance. The integration of nanotechnology, biomaterials, and targeted approaches has paved the way for more precise and personalized therapies. As biomedical scientists and biotechnologists continue to explore and refine these novel drug delivery systems, the future of medicine holds immense potential for improved patient care and better treatment outcomes.

Artificial Intelligence and Machine Learning in Drug Discovery

In recent years, the fields of Artificial Intelligence (AI) and Machine Learning (ML) have revolutionized various industries, and the field of drug discovery is no exception. This subchapter explores the exciting advancements in AI and ML techniques and their impact on the discovery and development of new medicines. Designed for a wide audience, particularly those interested in Biomedical Science and Biotechnology, this subchapter aims to provide a comprehensive overview of how these technologies are transforming the landscape of drug discovery.

Traditionally, the process of discovering new drugs has been a time-consuming and expensive endeavor, often taking years and costing billions of dollars. However, with the advent of AI and ML, scientists now have access to powerful tools that can expedite this process and improve the success rate of drug discovery.

One of the key applications of AI and ML in drug discovery is in the identification of potential drug targets. By analyzing vast amounts of biological data, including genomic and proteomic data, AI algorithms can identify specific molecules or proteins that play a crucial role in disease progression. This information can then be used to design drugs that target these molecules, offering a more precise and personalized approach to treatment.

Furthermore, AI and ML techniques can also be used to predict the efficacy and safety of potential drug candidates. By analyzing historical data on drug responses and adverse effects, these algorithms can identify patterns and make predictions on the likelihood of success or potential side effects. This allows researchers to prioritize the most promising candidates and reduce the number of failed experiments, saving both time and resources.

Additionally, AI and ML can be utilized to optimize the drug formulation and delivery process. By analyzing the physicochemical properties of drug molecules, these algorithms can suggest the most effective formulation and delivery methods to enhance drug efficacy and patient compliance.

While AI and ML have shown great promise in drug discovery, it is important to acknowledge their limitations. The algorithms are only as good as the data they are trained on, and biases in the data can lead to biased predictions. Additionally, the ethical implications of using AI in drug discovery, such as data privacy and ownership, need to be carefully considered.

In conclusion, the integration of AI and ML in drug discovery has the potential to revolutionize the field, accelerating the development of new medicines and improving patient outcomes. By harnessing the power of these technologies, scientists can now leverage vast amounts of data and make more informed decisions throughout the drug discovery process. However, it is crucial to ensure responsible and ethical use of AI and ML to maximize their benefits and minimize the risks associated with these technologies.

Chapter 10: Ethical Considerations in Medicinal Research

Informed Consent and Ethical Guidelines

In the field of biomedical science and biotechnology, the development and testing of new drugs and therapies play a crucial role in improving the health and well-being of individuals. However, it is equally important to ensure that these advancements are achieved ethically and with due consideration for the rights and safety of human subjects involved in clinical trials. This subchapter explores the concept of informed consent and the ethical guidelines that govern drug discovery and development.

Informed consent is a cornerstone of ethical medical research. It involves obtaining the voluntary agreement of individuals to participate in research studies after they have been provided with all relevant information regarding the study, including potential risks, benefits, and alternatives. Informed consent ensures that individuals have the autonomy to make decisions about their participation in research, based on their understanding of the study's purpose and potential consequences.

In biomedical science and biotechnology, ethical guidelines are in place to protect the rights and welfare of human subjects involved in research. These guidelines dictate that researchers must prioritize the well-being of participants and minimize any potential harm. Additionally, they require researchers to conduct rigorous risk assessments and adhere to stringent protocols to ensure the validity and reliability of their findings.

Ethical guidelines also emphasize the importance of transparency and accountability in research. Researchers must disclose any conflicts of interest, such as financial ties to pharmaceutical companies, to maintain the integrity of the research process. Furthermore, the guidelines stress the need for ongoing monitoring and review of research studies to ensure that they continue to meet ethical standards throughout their duration.

The subchapter will delve into the history and development of informed consent and ethical guidelines in the field of drug discovery and development. It will explore landmark cases and ethical dilemmas that have shaped these guidelines and discuss how they have evolved over time. It will also highlight the role of regulatory bodies, such as the Food and Drug Administration (FDA) in the United States, in enforcing these guidelines and safeguarding the rights of research participants.

By understanding the principles of informed consent and ethical guidelines, individuals in the fields of biomedical science and biotechnology can contribute to the responsible and ethical advancement of drug discovery and development. This subchapter aims to provide readers with a comprehensive overview of these essential concepts and their significance in the pursuit of scientific progress.

Animal Testing and Alternatives

In the field of biomedical science and biotechnology, the use of animals for testing purposes has long been a controversial topic. Animal testing has played a crucial role in the development of new medicines and treatments, but concerns about animal welfare and the reliability of results have led to the exploration of alternative methods.

Animal testing has been essential in understanding the safety and efficacy of potential drugs before they are administered to human subjects. By using animals as models, researchers can observe the effects of a drug on a living organism, providing valuable information about its potential benefits and potential side effects. This knowledge is crucial in drug discovery and development, as it helps scientists fine-tune formulations and dosages to maximize both safety and effectiveness.

However, the use of animals in testing has faced criticism due to ethical concerns. Many argue that subjecting animals to potentially harmful substances is cruel and unnecessary. In response to these concerns, researchers have been actively exploring alternative methods that can replace or reduce the reliance on animal testing.

One notable alternative is the use of in vitro models, where experiments are conducted using cells or tissues in a lab setting. This approach allows scientists to observe the effects of drugs on specific cells or tissues, providing valuable insights into drug interactions and potential toxicities. In vitro models offer several advantages, including reduced costs, faster results, and the ability to mimic specific human conditions more accurately.

Another alternative is the use of computer models and simulations, known as in silico testing. Virtual models can simulate the interactions between drugs and target molecules, providing valuable predictions about drug efficacy and potential side effects. In silico testing is a cost-effective and time-efficient method that allows researchers to test a wide range of drug candidates in a short amount of time.

The development of microfluidic devices, commonly referred to as "organs-on-chips," has also shown promise as an alternative to animal testing. These devices contain living cells that mimic the structure and function of human organs, allowing researchers to study drug effects in a more physiologically relevant environment. Organs-on-chips can provide valuable data on drug metabolism, toxicity, and efficacy, reducing the need for animal testing.

While alternative methods show great promise, it is important to note that they are not yet able to fully replace animal testing. They are currently used as complementary tools alongside animal studies to provide a more comprehensive understanding of drug effects. However, as technology continues to advance, it is likely that these alternatives will play an increasingly significant role in drug discovery and development, ultimately reducing the need for animal testing.

In conclusion, the field of biomedical science and biotechnology is actively exploring alternatives to animal testing. The ethical concerns surrounding animal welfare and the need for more reliable testing methods have led to the development of in vitro models, in silico testing, and organs-on-chips. While these alternatives are not yet capable of completely replacing animal testing, they offer valuable insights into drug interactions and potential toxicities. As technology continues to advance, it is hopeful that these alternatives will continue to evolve, ultimately leading to more reliable and ethical methods in drug discovery and development.

Balancing Benefits and Risks in Drug Development

In the realm of biomedical science and biotechnology, the development of new drugs is a complex and critical process. It involves extensive research, rigorous testing, and a delicate balance between maximizing benefits and minimizing risks. This subchapter explores the challenges and considerations that go into this balancing act, shedding light on the fascinating world of drug development.

The primary goal of drug development is to improve human health and well-being. However, this noble pursuit is not without its challenges. Scientists and researchers must carefully evaluate the potential benefits of a new drug against the inherent risks it may pose to patients. Balancing these factors requires a comprehensive understanding of the drug's mechanism of action, potential side effects, and overall efficacy.

The journey of a drug from the laboratory to the pharmacy shelf often begins with preclinical studies. Here, scientists meticulously investigate the drug's safety, dosage, and potential biological targets. Animal models are commonly used to assess the drug's effectiveness and potential side effects. These experiments provide valuable insights into the drug's pharmacokinetics and toxicology, allowing researchers to make informed decisions about its further development.

Once a drug demonstrates promising results in preclinical studies, it moves into clinical trials. These trials involve human volunteers and are conducted in multiple phases to assess the drug's safety, dosing, and efficacy. They are carefully designed to minimize risks to participants while gathering robust data on the drug's benefits and potential side effects. Ethical considerations, such as informed consent and patient safety, are paramount throughout the process.

Balancing benefits and risks in drug development also requires regulatory oversight. Government agencies, such as the Food and Drug Administration (FDA), play a crucial role in ensuring that drugs meet rigorous standards of safety and efficacy before they can be approved for public use. This regulatory framework adds an extra layer of protection for patients, ensuring that new drugs undergo rigorous scrutiny before reaching the market.

In conclusion, balancing benefits and risks in drug development is a complex and essential process in the field of biomedical science and biotechnology. Scientists, researchers, and regulatory agencies work together to evaluate the potential benefits of a new drug against its inherent risks. Through preclinical studies, clinical trials, and regulatory oversight, the goal is to maximize the benefits of new drugs while minimizing potential harm to patients. This delicate balance is crucial to advancing medical science and improving the lives of individuals worldwide.

Chapter 11: Conclusion: The Impact of Medicines on Society

Medical Breakthroughs and Improved Patient Outcomes

In the ever-evolving field of medicine, breakthroughs and innovations continue to shape the way we approach healthcare. From groundbreaking discoveries to cutting-edge technologies, medical advancements have played a pivotal role in improving patient outcomes and transforming the landscape of biomedical science and biotechnology. This subchapter explores some of the most significant medical breakthroughs that have revolutionized patient care and contributed to better treatment options.

One of the most remarkable medical breakthroughs in recent times is the development of personalized medicine. This approach takes into account an individual's genetic makeup, lifestyle, and environmental factors to tailor treatment plans specifically for that patient. By using genetic tests and advanced technologies, doctors can now predict a patient's response to certain medications, reducing the risk of adverse reactions and optimizing the effectiveness of treatment. Personalized medicine has not only improved patient outcomes but also opened up new avenues for targeted therapies and precision medicine.

Another significant breakthrough is the advent of regenerative medicine. This field focuses on harnessing the body's own regenerative capabilities to repair and replace damaged tissues and organs. Stem cell therapy, for instance, holds immense promise for treating conditions such as Parkinson's disease, diabetes, and spinal cord injuries. By utilizing stem cells to regenerate damaged tissues, researchers are pushing the boundaries of what is possible in terms of restoring function and improving the quality of life for patients.

In the realm of biotechnology, the development of monoclonal antibodies has revolutionized the treatment of various diseases. These laboratory-produced antibodies mimic the immune system's natural response to infections, tumors, and other threats. Monoclonal antibodies have been successfully used in the treatment of cancer, autoimmune disorders, and infectious diseases, offering new hope to patients who previously had limited treatment options.

Furthermore, the integration of artificial intelligence (AI) and machine learning algorithms in healthcare has paved the way for more accurate diagnoses and personalized treatment plans. AI-powered tools can analyze vast amounts of patient data, identify patterns, and make predictions that assist clinicians in making informed decisions. This not only saves time but also improves patient outcomes by providing more precise and tailored treatments.

As medical breakthroughs continue to unfold, the future of healthcare holds immense promise. With advancements in fields such as personalized medicine, regenerative medicine, biotechnology, and AI, patients can look forward to improved outcomes, enhanced quality of life, and a new era of healthcare that is more precise, efficient, and patient-centric.

Whether you're a healthcare professional, a scientist, or simply a curious individual, exploring these medical breakthroughs is key to understanding the transformative power of science and its potential to revolutionize the way we approach medicine. By staying informed and embracing these advancements, we can all contribute to a future where improved patient outcomes and better healthcare are accessible to everyone.

Challenges and Opportunities in Drug Discovery

In the fast-paced world of biomedical science and biotechnology, the field of drug discovery holds immense promise and potential. It represents the constant pursuit of finding new treatments and cures for diseases that afflict humanity. However, drug discovery also comes with its fair share of challenges and opportunities that researchers and scientists must navigate on their quest for innovative medicines.

One of the primary challenges in drug discovery is the complex nature of diseases themselves. Many diseases involve intricate biological processes and pathways that are not fully understood. Unraveling these mysteries requires extensive research and experimentation, often taking years or even decades. Furthermore, diseases can vary greatly between individuals, making it difficult to develop a one-size-fits-all treatment. This necessitates the need for personalized medicine, where drugs are tailored to individual patients based on their genetic makeup and specific disease characteristics.

Another challenge lies in the identification and validation of drug targets. Drug targets are specific molecules or proteins within the body that can be manipulated to treat a disease. However, identifying suitable targets is a complex task that requires a deep understanding of disease biology. Once a target is identified, it must undergo rigorous validation to ensure its relevance and potential as a therapeutic target. This process involves extensive testing in preclinical models and clinical trials to determine the drug's efficacy and safety.

The cost and time required for drug discovery pose significant challenges as well. Developing a new drug from concept to market can take upwards of 10-15 years and cost billions of dollars. This lengthy and expensive process is due to the rigorous testing and regulatory requirements that ensure the safety and effectiveness of drugs. Additionally, many potential drug candidates fail at various stages of development, further increasing the time and cost involved.

However, amidst these challenges, there are also numerous opportunities in drug discovery. Advances in technology, such as high-throughput screening and computational modeling, have revolutionized the drug discovery process. These tools allow for the rapid screening of large libraries of compounds and the prediction of their potential efficacy, reducing the time and cost of drug discovery.

Furthermore, the emergence of new fields like genomics and proteomics provides exciting opportunities for drug discovery. These disciplines allow researchers to gain a deeper understanding of disease mechanisms at a molecular level, enabling the identification of novel drug targets and the development of more precise therapies.

In conclusion, drug discovery is a field filled with challenges and opportunities. While the complexity of diseases, the identification of drug targets, and the cost and time required present significant obstacles, advances in technology and the ever-expanding knowledge of disease biology offer hope for novel and effective treatments. By addressing these challenges and capitalizing on the opportunities, researchers in the field of drug discovery continue to make remarkable strides towards improving human health and well-being.

The Role of Collaboration and Innovation in Medicinal Research

In the fast-paced world of biomedical science and biotechnology, collaboration and innovation play a pivotal role in driving breakthroughs in medicinal research. In this subchapter, we will explore the significance of collaboration and innovation, and how they contribute to the advancement of drug discovery and development.

Collaboration, both within and across disciplines, is essential for tackling complex challenges in medicinal research. By bringing together experts from various fields such as biology, chemistry, pharmacology, and clinical medicine, collaborative efforts can harness the collective knowledge and skills of individuals, leading to faster and more efficient progress. Furthermore, collaboration between academia, pharmaceutical companies, and government institutions fosters a diverse and multidimensional approach to problem-solving, promoting the exchange of ideas and resources.

One of the key benefits of collaboration is the ability to pool resources, including funding, infrastructure, and expertise. This allows researchers to conduct larger-scale studies, access cutting-edge technologies, and share data, ultimately accelerating the pace of discovery. Collaborative efforts also promote transparency and reproducibility, as multiple researchers can independently verify and validate findings, ensuring the reliability and credibility of research outcomes.

Innovation is equally crucial in medicinal research, as it drives the development of novel therapies and treatment approaches. Innovations in technology, such as high-throughput screening, genome editing, and computational modeling, have revolutionized the drug discovery process, enabling researchers to identify potential drug candidates more efficiently. Moreover, advancements in imaging techniques, such as positron emission tomography (PET) and magnetic resonance imaging (MRI), have enhanced our understanding of disease mechanisms and the effects of drugs on the human body.

Innovation also extends beyond the laboratory, as researchers explore new ways to eimaging techniques, such as positron emission tomography (PET) and magnetic resonance imaging (MRI), have enhanced our understanding of disease mechanisms ngage with patients and the wider community. Patient-centered research initiatives, for instance, involve patients in the decision-making process, ensuring that their needs and perspectives are considered. This not only enhances the relevance and impact of research but also fosters a sense of ownership and empowerment among patients.

In conclusion, collaboration and innovation are integral to the field of medicinal research, driving progress and transforming the landscape of drug discovery and development. By fostering collaboration across disciplines and institutions, and embracing innovative approaches, researchers can overcome complex challenges, accelerate discovery, and ultimately improve patient outcomes. Whether you are a scientist, a healthcare professional, or simply interested in the field, understanding the role of collaboration and innovation in medicinal research is essential to stay abreast of the latest advancements and contribute to the future of healthcare.

www.ingramcontent.com/pod-product-compliance
Lightning Source LLC
LaVergne TN
LVHW052002060526
838201LV00059B/3788